Taylor Lautner

By Robin Johnson

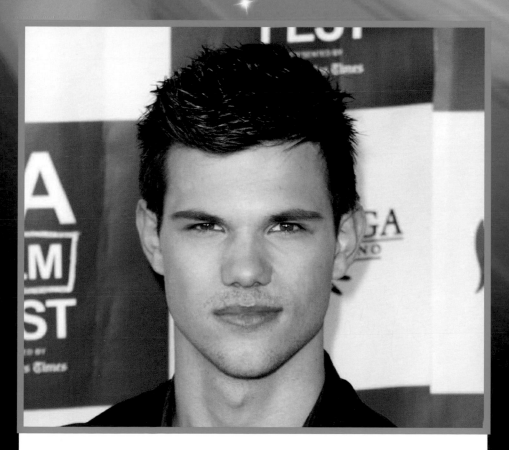

Crabtree Publishing Company

www.crabtreebooks.com

Crabtree Publishing Company
www.crabtreebooks.com

Author: Robin Johnson
Publishing plan research and development:
   Sean Charlebois, Reagan Miller
   Crabtree Publishing Company
Project coordinator: Kathy Middleton
Photo research: Crystal Sikkens
Editor: Lynn Peppas
Designer: Ken Wright
**Production coordinator and prepress
   technician:** Ken Wright
Print coordinator: Katherine Berti

Photographs:
Alamy: © AF archive: pages 12, 17
Getty Images: WireImage: pages 8, 9, 11, 19;
   NBC: pages 13, 25
Keystone Press: ©Entertainment Pictures:
   page 14; ZUMAPRESS.com: page 16;
   © FAME Pictures: page 20; wenn.com:
   page 26; © MAVRIXPHOTO.COM: page 27
© Face to Face/Photoshot: page 18
Shutterstock: Featureflash: cover, pages 4, 5,
   6, 10, 24; Photo Works: page 1; s_bukley:
   pages 7, 15; RoidRanger: page 21 (top); Joe
   Seer: pages 21 (bottom), 23; Jaguar PS:
   page 22; Helga Esteb: page 28

Every effort has been made to trace copyright holders and to
obtain their permission for use of copyright material. The
authors and publishers would be pleased to rectify any error or
omission in future editions. All the Internet addresses given in
this book were correct at the time of going to press. The author
and publishers regret any inconvenience caused if addresses
have changed or sites have ceased to exist, but can accept no
responsibility for any such changes.

Library and Archives Canada Cataloguing in Publication

CIP available at Library and Archives Canada

Library of Congress Cataloging-in-Publication Data

Johnson, Robin (Robin R.)
   Taylor Lautner / by Robin Johnson.
      p. cm. -- (Superstars!)
   Includes index.
   ISBN 978-0-7787-7619-2 (reinforced library binding : alk. paper)
-- ISBN 978-0-7787-7632-1 (pbk. : alk. paper) -- ISBN 978-1-4271-
7921-0 (electronic pdf) -- ISBN 978-1-4271-8036-0 (electronic html)
   1. Lautner, Taylor, 1992---Juvenile literature. 2. Actors--United
States--Biography--Juvenile literature. I. Title.

PN2287.L2855J86 2012
791.4302'8092--dc23
[B]
                                                 2012033408

Crabtree Publishing Company
www.crabtreebooks.com   1-800-387-7650

Printed in Canada/102012/MA20120817

Published in Canada
Crabtree Publishing
616 Welland Ave.
St. Catharines, ON
L2M 5V6

Published in the United States
Crabtree Publishing
PMB 59051
350 Fifth Avenue, 59th Floor
New York, New York 10118

Published in the United Kingdom
Crabtree Publishing
Maritime House
Basin Road North, Hove
BN41 1WR

Published in Australia
Crabtree Publishing
3 Charles Street
Coburg North
VIC 3058

CONTENTS

Team Taylor 4

A Fighting Chance 8

Teen Wolf 14

Tay Today 22

Timeline 29

Glossary 30

Find Out More 31

Index 32

Words that are defined in the glossary are in
bold type the first time they appear in the text.

Team Taylor

Taylor Lautner is the hottest teen wolf ever to hit the big screen. He howled at the moon in the smash hit "Twilight" films that captured the imaginations of tweens and teens worldwide. Taylor's role as Jacob Black—a nice guy turned vicious **werewolf**—rocketed the young actor to superstardom. There is much more to Taylor, however, than a killer smile and a thick coat of fur.

CRY WOLF

Taylor became famous for playing a werewolf in the *Twilight* films. Werewolves are fictional human creatures who have the ability to change into wolves. Werewolves are said to appear at night when the moon is full.

Fan Fave

Taylor is popular with preteens and teens around the world. He has won Teen Choice Awards, Kids' Choice Awards, and People's Choice Awards for his performances in the *Twilight* series. Taylor has also won awards for his smile and "fresh face," for being the "Hottest Hottie," and for being the "Favorite Buttkicker" to hit the big screen.

Twilight stars Taylor Lautner (left), Kristen Stewart, and Robert Pattinson clean up at the 2009 MTV Movie Awards.

Tay Day

Taylor—who is sometimes called "TLaut," "Tay," or "Tay—Tay"—has also starred in a number of other popular feature films. He got his first big break at the age of 13 when he landed a shark. Taylor was cast in the lead role of *The Adventures of Sharkboy and Lavagirl in 3–D*. The children's adventure film showed the world that Taylor had star power. Taylor recently appeared in the hit comedy *Valentine's Day* and starred in the action film *Abduction*. And this young actor is just getting started.

Body of Work

Taylor takes good care of his body. He trains in martial arts regularly. He follows a careful diet plan. He does not smoke, drink, or use drugs.

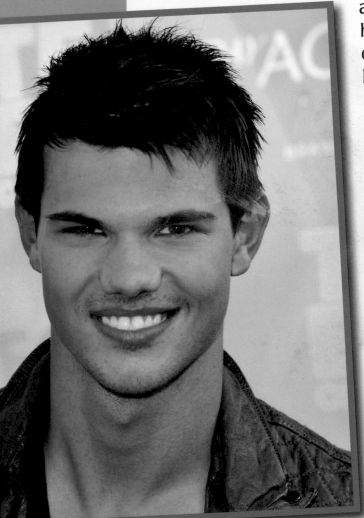

Taylor's healthy living and natural charms have made him one of Hollywood's hottest leading men. He is admired for his bronze skin, deep brown eyes, and dazzling white smile. He is also famous for his six-pack abs. Taylor took off his shirt for the *Twilight* films and became an instant teen idol. Girls around the world think he is abs—olutely gorgeous!

He Said It

"We've met many different fans: the criers, who come around quite often; the **hyperventilators** who stop breathing and have to have a medic come. We've definitely seen some passion."
—Interview *magazine, August 2009*

Wolf in Chic Clothing

Taylor won the Teen Choice Award for being a "Red Carpet Fashion Icon." Fans love to see what the 5-foot 10-inch (1.79 m) actor is wearing both on and off the red carpet. Taylor describes his style as "not too fashiony, but cool and comfortable" with "a little edge to it." His favorite thing to wear is a leather jacket.

Taylor is a stylish dresser who rocks jeans and a t-shirt or a fitted suit.

TOUGH TAYLOR

Taylor is not just another pretty face. He is a highly skilled martial artist with a **black belt** in karate. Taylor is also a three—time Junior World Karate Champion!

A Fighting Chance

Taylor was driven to succeed from a young age. He began fighting on the karate mat when he was just six years old. Soon, he was fighting for parts in movies and television shows. After several years and a few bit parts, Taylor finally got his first big break.

Taylor takes his sister to the movies for the *Cheaper by the Dozen 2* premiere.

A Star is Born

Taylor Daniel Lautner was born on February 11, 1992, in Grand Rapids, Michigan. He was the first child for the young, middle–class couple Daniel and Deborah Lautner. Six years later, Taylor's sister Makena was born. Taylor and his sister were raised in the Roman Catholic religion, in a loving and supportive household. They grew up in a small town in Michigan called Hudsonville. Although the Lautners lived far from Hollywood, Taylor's parents were willing to do whatever it took to make their son's dreams come true.

Karate Kid

Taylor took up karate at the age of six. He was quick, athletic, and very **disciplined**. He trained hard and soon began taking home prizes in the sport. A year later, Taylor met Michael Chaturantabut at a martial arts tournament. Michael is a world-champion martial artist, stuntman, and actor. He often goes by the name Mike Chat. Mike invited Taylor to summer camp, then offered to train him. Taylor trained hard—as much as four hours a day—and soon earned his black belt in karate.

Young Taylor busts a move at a 2005 film **premiere**.

World Champion

In 2000, Taylor was chosen to represent the United States on the national karate team. He competed in the "12 and under" division of the World Karate Federation Championships. Although eight-year-old Taylor was much younger and smaller than the other kids in his division, he dominated the event. In fact, Taylor became the Junior World Forms and Weapons Champion! By the time he was 12 years old, talented Taylor had won three Junior World Championships in karate.

Flying High

Taylor trained with Mike for several years. Mike saw **potential** in his young student, and not just on the mat. Mike—who had played the Blue Ranger in the Power Rangers TV show—encouraged Taylor to try his hand at acting. Taylor **auditioned** for a Burger King commercial. He did not get the part, but he did get a taste for acting. Mike set Taylor up with an **agent** in Los Angeles. For a few years, Taylor flew across the country from Michigan to L.A. for auditions.

FREQUENT FLYER

Taylor's father was a commercial airline pilot so it was easy for Taylor to fly from place to place for auditions. Taylor would go to an audition first thing in the morning and still be home in time for school that day!

He Said It

"I heard, 'No, no, no, no,' so many times. From karate, I had the confidence and drive to push myself."
—*Interview in Michigan's* Grand Rapids Press

Hooray for Hollywood

In 2002, the furniture factory where Taylor's mother worked closed down. The Lautners decided to move to California so young Taylor could make it big. They settled in Valencia, a **suburb** of Hollywood. Over the next few years, Taylor landed small parts in movies and television shows. He appeared in the sci-fi movie *Shadow Fury* and the comedy film *Cheaper by the Dozen 2*. He scored small roles in the television series *The Bernie Mac Show*, *My Wife and Kids*, and *Summerland*. Taylor also did some voice acting for the cartoons *Danny Phantom*, *Duck Dodgers*, and *What's New, Scooby–Doo?*

Taylor hits the red carpet for the **premiere** of his first feature film.

Swimming With Sharks

In 2005, Taylor got his first big break. The 13-year-old was cast in the children's fantasy movie *The Adventures of Sharkboy and Lavagirl in 3-D*. Taylor played the junior superhero Sharkboy, a kid who was raised by sharks. Sharkboy has gills, fins, and very sharp teeth. He is also a strong swimmer and—like Taylor—a highly skilled fighter. Taylor acted swimmingly in his first major role, earning a Young Artist Award nomination for his performance. He did not win the award, but he did capture the attention of young moviegoers.

Taylor shows he has star power in *The Adventures of Sharkboy and Lavagirl in 3-D*.

School Days

When he was not working, Taylor loved to play sports. He played football and baseball on his school teams for about eight years. He also did hip-hop and jazz dance. Taylor stayed in public school until grade ten. At that time he left school to pursue his acting career full-time. Taylor later wrote a **proficiency exam** and graduated from high school.

His Own Worst Enemy

In 2008, Taylor landed a starring role in a new television drama series. The show was called *My Own Worst Enemy*. It followed the double life of a secret agent and family man, played by American actor Christian Slater. Taylor played the role of Christian's son, Jack Spivey, in the series. Unfortunately, the cast of *My Own Worst Enemy* had the worst luck. The series was canceled after only nine episodes. Fortunately, Taylor's career was about to take off in another direction.

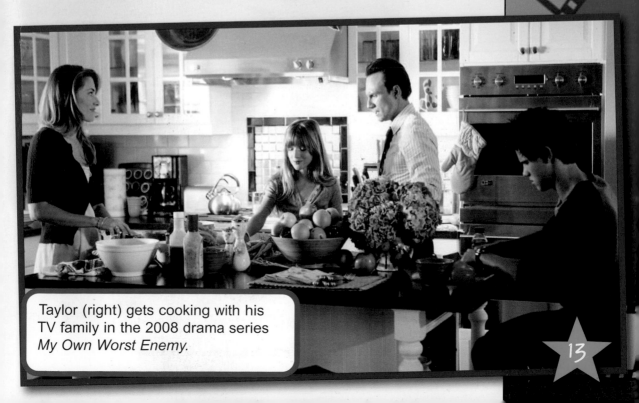

Taylor (right) gets cooking with his TV family in the 2008 drama series *My Own Worst Enemy*.

Teen Wolf

Taylor cried wolf—and packs of screaming fans answered the call. Although Taylor had only four scenes in the megahit movie, *Twilight*—and spoke a total of only 239 words—the role rocketed the young actor to fame.

jacob

twilight

Love Triangle

Twilight is a romantic fantasy film about an unlikely love triangle. Bella Swan (played by American actress Kristen Stewart) is a sweet, shy 17-year-old girl. She moves to Forks, Washington, and meets a mysterious boy named Edward Cullen (played by British actor Robert Pattinson). Bella's best friend, Jacob, tries to warn her about her dangerous crush—and starts to develop feelings for Bella in the process. By the time Bella realizes that Edward is a blood-sucking **vampire**, she is already deeply in love with him. Their difficult relationship forms the basis of both the film and the hit book that inspired it.

Monster Hit

The *Twilight* movie is based on the bestselling vampire romance, YA (young-adult) novel by Stephenie Meyer. The book became an instant hit when it hit stores in October 2005. **Sequels** to the book—entitled *New Moon, Eclipse,* and *Breaking Dawn*—were just as popular. When the first film of the series was released on November 21, 2008, *Twilight* already had a huge and **passionate** fan base. Preteens and teens rushed to movie theaters—many camping out days before the film opened—to see their favorite characters brought to life on the big screen. *Twilight* was a monster hit, making nearly $36 million the day it opened!

Taylor walks the red carpet in style at the Los Angeles premiere of *Twilight*.

He Said It

"It's the weirdest thing. Nobody really saw it coming. I mean, we knew we were making a movie of a very popular book, but we didn't know how well it was going to do. When it opened, it exploded, and that was not something any of us saw coming."
—*Taylor describing the opening of* Twilight *in* Interview *magazine, August 2009*

Meet Jacob Black

Taylor plays the role of Jacob "Jake" Black in the *Twilight* film. Jacob has dark skin, dark eyes, and long, black hair. He is a friendly, happy-go-lucky, clumsy, 15-year-old boy. In the *Twilight* book, Bella describes Jacob as "someone I could easily be friends with." As the series progresses, however, Bella comes to see Jacob as "sort of beautiful," and sort of more than just a friend.

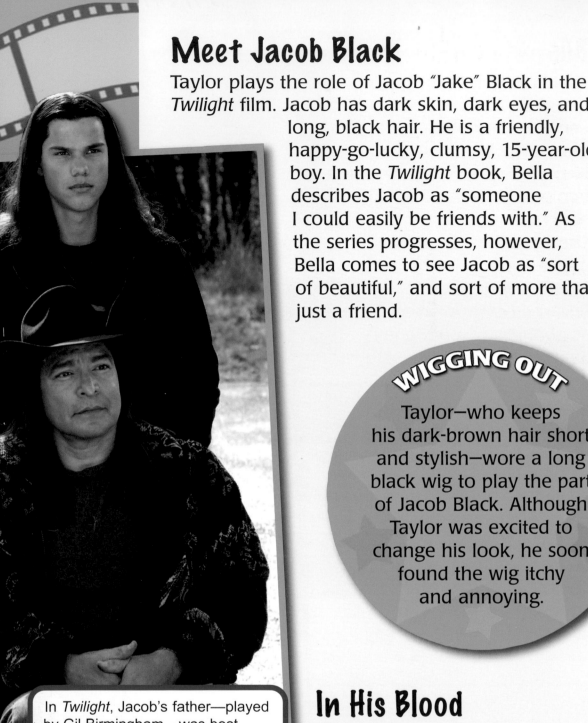

In *Twilight*, Jacob's father—played by Gil Birmingham—was best friends with Bella Swan's father.

WIGGING OUT

Taylor—who keeps his dark-brown hair short and stylish—wore a long black wig to play the part of Jacob Black. Although Taylor was excited to change his look, he soon found the wig itchy and annoying.

In His Blood

Jacob Black lives on a **reservation** in La Push, Washington. He is a member of the Quileute tribe, a Native American people in western Washington State. Like Jacob, Taylor is part Native American. Taylor has distant Ottawa and Potawatomi roots. His other ancestors were German, French, and Dutch.

Bigger and Better

In *New Moon*, the sequel to *Twilight*, Jacob's body goes through changes. He grows up and becomes very strong and muscular. The new body was a challenge for slim young Taylor. In fact, the film's producers almost cast a new actor to play the part! They were considering hiring big, buff actor Michael Copon for the role. *Twilight* fans were not impressed. They protested and fought to keep Taylor in the series. Taylor was determined to keep the part, too. He hired a personal trainer and worked out for two and a half hours a day. He trained for nine months and packed on 30 pounds (14 kg) of muscle! Taylor's hard work in the gym paid off. He auditioned for the part of Jacob Black—again— and kept his job.

Jacob Black gets bigger and better as the *Twilight* series continues

He Said It

"I'm very happy to announce that Taylor Lautner will be playing Jacob Black in *New Moon*… It was my first instinct that Taylor was, is, and should be Jacob."
—*New Moon* director Chris Weitz on StephenieMeyer.com

Taking Shape

In *New Moon*, Edward leaves Bella so his bloodthirsty family will not harm her. Bella finds comfort in the company of her friend, Jacob. As the story progresses, Jacob undergoes a surprising transformation. He becomes a **shape–shifter** who takes on the form of a giant wolf. As a werewolf, Jacob has superhuman strength and speed–and a lot of fur. In human form, Jacob is very fast, strong, and **agile**. He is also very tall and muscular.

New Moon Rising

The Twilight Saga: New Moon hit theaters on November 20, 2009. Devoted fans of the series were dressed and ready for it! They bought tickets weeks ahead and lined up for days to see the big stars on the big screen. The hit sequel earned more than $72 million in the United States and Canada on opening day. The film also earned Taylor a place in the hearts of werewolf–loving preteens and teens everywhere.

Taylor and Kristen Stewart won the 2010 Kids' Choice Award for being the cutest couple in the *New Moon* film.

Team Players

Fans of the *Twilight* series are called Twi-hards, Twi-fans, Twilighters, or fanpires. They know everything about the books and films—including who would be the best monster for Bella! Members of "Team Jacob" think that real men don't sparkle, since vampire Edward sparkles in the sunlight. These fans believe that werewolf Jacob is the real head of the pack. Members of "Team Edward" wish Bella a vampire love to last forever. "Team Switzerland" refuses to take sides. These fans love both handsome creatures!

Valentine's Day Date

In early 2010, Taylor found time for a special Valentine's Day date. He had a small role in the star-studded romantic comedy *Valentine's Day*. In the film, Taylor plays the part of a high school athlete named Willy Harrington. Willy is in love with a girl named Felicia Miller, played by country pop superstar Taylor Swift. Sparks flew between the two Taylors in the film (who dated for a few months in 2009). In fact, the couple was nominated for Teen Choice Awards for having the best chemistry and sharing the best kiss on *Valentine's Day*!

LONE WOLF

After the two Taylors broke up, Taylor Swift wrote a country song about her same-name sweetie. In "Back to December," she sings, "I miss your tan skin, your sweet smile, so good to me, so right."

Kristen Stewart is torn between two handsome men at the Eclipse premiere

Black is Back

Taylor and the rest of the *Twilight* cast returned to theaters with a bang on June 30, 2010. The *Twilight Saga: Eclipse* smashed attendance records for a Wednesday opening, earning $68.5 million that night. In the third film of the series, Jacob and his wolf pack join forces with Edward and his vampire family to protect Bella from danger. Bella is torn between Jacob and Edward in the dangerous love triangle that takes shape. *Eclipse's* mix of romance and action thrilled fans of the series but not critics. In fact, all the *Twilight* films have received mixed reviews. Even bad reviews could not keep Twi-hards from flocking to theaters in record numbers.

Tay Today

Today, Taylor continues to heat up the big screen with his gorgeous smile and well–defined muscles. He recently returned as Jacob Black in the fourth *Twilight* movie, with the final film of the series just around the corner. Taylor has also taken on less furry roles in a variety of feature films.

Taylor lights up the nighttime premiere of *Breaking Dawn Part 1*

Breaking Dawn

The Twilight Saga: Breaking Dawn Part 1 hit theaters on November 18, 2011. The final—and longest—book in the series was divided into two feature films. Like the other movies in the series, *Breaking Dawn Part 1* shattered box office records. It made $30.25 million at its midnight opening, and then went on to make more than $705 million! In the film, Taylor returns as wolf boy Jacob Black. Jacob is heartbroken when Bella marries Edward, has his vampire child, and is transformed into a vampire. Jacob says, "I know how this ends and I'm not sticking around to watch."

Breaking Dawn Again

Twilight fans are sure to stick around to watch the fifth and final film in the series. In *Breaking Dawn Part 2*, Bella will learn how to live as a vampire and protect her daughter from harm. The film is set for release on November 16, 2012. With teen idol Taylor starring in the film, *Breaking Dawn Part 2* will likely break box office records—and more than a few young hearts.

Mackenzie Foy plays Bella and Edward's daughter Renesmee in the *Breaking Dawn* films. Jacob plays a big role in Renesmee's life.

He Said It

"The goal for us has always been to live up to the expectation of the books. Because that's what the fans fell in love with. These fans were just as passionate before the movies even started. They fell in love with the characters that Stephenie Meyer created, so our goal all along was just to please the fans who had this very specific picture of what they wanted to see on the screen. Because that's who we're making these movies for."

—Taylor discussing *Breaking Dawn Part 2* at the 2012 Teen Choice Awards

Action Hero

In the fall of 2011, Taylor was ready for action! He played the lead role of Nathan Harper in the thriller *Abduction*. In the film, Nathan discovers that his parents are not who they seem. He begins a journey to learn the truth about his life—and ends up running for his life instead. *Abduction* is packed with action, and athletic Taylor did most of his own stunts in the film. Critics hated the movie, but Taylor's fans loved it. They honored him with the 2012 Teen Choice Award for a movie actor in an action film.

Taylor thrills fans at the premiere of the thriller *Abduction*.

All Grown Up

Taylor is growing up—and taking a turn at comedy. The young actor will soon appear in a feature film called *Grown Ups 2*. The movie is a sequel to the popular comedy film *Grown Ups*. In the sequel, Taylor will play a college boy named Andy. The movie—which stars Adam Sandler and Salma Hayek—is set to open on July 12, 2013.

MEET MARIANNA

Taylor first showed his funny side when he hosted the comedy show Saturday Night Live in 2009. He wore a "Team Edward" t-shirt and pretended to be a pretty young superfan named Marianna.

Taylor is shown here playing Marianna on *Saturday Night Live*. He has a picture of Edward from the *Twilight* movies covering his face.

Family Guy

Taylor may be growing up, but he still lives at home. He lives with his parents and younger sister in Valencia, California. The wealthy superstar could afford to buy a mansion or two—he is one of the highest-paid young actors in Hollywood—but Taylor prefers to live with his family. He said, "The thing I love is that my home life hasn't changed. I still help out with the garbage. I still help out with the lawn."

Friends and More

Taylor is a homebody when he is not on the movie set. He says he's "not the guy who likes to go out so much." Taylor enjoys just hanging out at home with friends or going over to a friend's place. He does, however, like to take his girlfriends out for a good time. Besides Taylor Swift, Taylor Lautner has also been romantically linked to actress Lily Collins and actress/pop singer Selena Gomez. It seems the handsome actor hasn't met his match yet, though.

Lily Collins co-starred with Taylor in the movie *Abduction*.

On the Ball

When Taylor is not fighting vampires or doing yard work, he loves to play and watch sports. His favorite sports are football and baseball. Taylor says that if he was not an actor, he would probably be an athlete. Taylor also enjoys writing and directing, and would love to work behind the camera some day. He is also interested in studying **psychology**, and he has already completed several courses at community college.

Taylor makes a diving catch at a celebrity beach football game.

He Said It

"I have a football with me a lot on set. It's comforting to me, even if that sounds really weird. I'm always carrying a football and playing catch with the cast and crew. Because when I'm at home, I'm always throwing it with my friends and family!" –Interview in *Seventeen* magazine, October 2011

27

Taylor Time

Taylor is sure to attack any new role with discipline and determination. Whether he howls at the moon as a dreamy werewolf or has moviegoers howling with laughter, Taylor continues to delight fans around the world. He is always changing and reinventing himself. Keep watching this talented young actor to see who—or what—Taylor shape-shifts into next.

He Said It

"This was a childhood dream of mine to be making movies… I love it. It's so much fun. I never thought I would be sitting here today. I'm extremely honored and blessed. I still have to pinch myself and tell myself it's real because it does feel like a dream."
—Interview on the *Today* show, September 21, 2011

Timeline

1992: Taylor Daniel Lautner is born on February 11 in Grand Rapids, Michigan.

1998: Taylor starts taking karate lessons.

2000: Taylor is chosen for the U.S. national karate team. He goes on to become a three-time Junior World Karate Champion.

2002: The Lautner family moves from Michigan to California so Taylor can pursue his acting career.

2003-2005: Taylor gets small parts and voice-only roles in a number of TV shows and movies.

2005: Taylor gets his first big break when he lands the lead in the children's film *The Adventures of Sharkboy and Lavagirl in 3–D*.

2008: Taylor lands a starring role in a new television drama series called *My Own Worst Enemy*. The series is canceled after only nine episodes.

2008: *Twilight* opens on November 21. Taylor plays Jacob Black in the wildly successful film.

2008: Taylor graduates from high school.

2009: *The Twilight Saga: New Moon* opens on November 20. Taylor returns in the series as a more muscular—and more monstrous—Jacob Black.

2010: Taylor has a small role in the romantic comedy *Valentine's Day*, playing opposite Taylor Swift.

2010: On June 30, Taylor returns to the big screen as wolf boy Jacob Black in *The Twilight Saga: Eclipse*.

2011: *Abduction* opens in theaters on September 23. Taylor plays the lead role in the action film.

2011: *The Twilight Saga: Breaking Dawn Part 1* hits theaters on November 18. Taylor returns as Jacob Black in the fourth film of the series.

2012: *The Twilight Saga: Breaking Dawn Part 2* hits theaters on November 16. Taylor plays Jacob Black in the final film of the smash series.

2013: Taylor takes a turn at comedy in the feature film *Grown Ups 2*. It opens in theaters on July 12.

Glossary

agent A person who acts on behalf of someone else

agile Able to move quickly and easily

audition To try out for a part by giving a short performance

black belt A cloth belt awarded to a karate expert

discipline To show control and work hard in training and other areas

hyperventilators People breathing harder and faster than is necessary

passionate Having strong feelings about someone or something

potential The ability to succeed in the future

premiere The first public showing of a movie or other show

proficiency exam A test that measures a student's knowledge of certain subjects

psychology The study of the human mind

reservation An area of land set aside for use by Native Americans

sequels Books or movies that continue the story told in a previous book or movie

shape-shifter Someone who can change their shape or form, such as a person who transforms into a wolf

suburb An area of houses on the edge of a city

vampire A dead person who acts like he or she is alive and must drink blood to survive

werewolf A person who changes into a wolf

Find Out More

Books

Baldwin, Garrett. *Bonded by Blood: Robert Pattinson and Taylor Lautner.* Plexus Publishing, 2010.

Griffin Llanas, Sheila. *Star Biographies: Taylor Lautner.* Capstone Press, 2012.

Nelson, Maria. *Rising Stars: Taylor Lautner.* Gareth Stevens Publishing, 2011.

Websites

Taylor Lautner Online
   http://taylorlautner.org/
A fan site devoted to Taylor Lautner

Taylor Lautner Source
   http://taylorlautnersource.com/
Your source for all things Taylor

Taylor Lautner.com
   http://taylor-lautner.com/
The premier Taylor Lautner fan site

The Twilight Saga
   http://thetwilightsaga.com/
The official website for *Twilight* fans

Index

auditions 10, 17

awards 5, 12, 18, 23, 24

Black, Jacob 4, 14, 16, 17, 18, 21, 22, 29

Chaturantabut, Mike 9, 10

Collins, Lily 26

education 13, 27, 29

family 8, 10, 11, 16, 26, 27

fans 5, 6, 7, 18, 19, 21

fashion sense 7

Gomez, Selena 26

karate 7, 8, 9, 29

love interests 14, 20, 26

martial arts 6, 7, 9

Meyer, Stephenie 15, 23

movies

   Abduction 5, 24, 26, 29

   Breaking Dawn Part 1 15, 22, 29

   Breaking Dawn Part 2 15, 23, 29

   Cheaper by the Dozen 2 8, 11

   Eclipse 15, 21, 29

   Grown Ups 2 25, 29

New Moon 15, 17, 18, 29

Shadow Fury 11

The Adventures of Sharkboy and Lavagirl in 3-D 5, 12, 29

Twilight 4, 5, 6, 14, 1 5, 21, 22, 29

Valentine's Day 5, 20, 29

My Own Worst Enemy (TV Show) 13, 29

Pattinson, Robert 5, 14, 21

sports 13, 27

Stewart, Kristen 5, 14, 21

Swift, Taylor 20, 26

Team Jacob 19

television shows 11, 13

ticket sales 15, 18, 21, 22

training 6, 17

Twi-hards 19, 21

Twilight series (books) 15, 16, 22, 23

voice acting 11, 29

werewolves 4, 18, 19, 21, 22, 28

About the Author

Robin Johnson is a freelance author and editor. She has written more than 20 nonfiction children's books, including *Kristen Stewart*, *Robert Pattinson*, and *Katy Perry*. When she isn't working, she divides her time between renovating her home with her husband, taking her two sons to hockey practice, and exploring the back roads of North America.